I0088166

PRESCRIPTION

for

BREAKTHROUGH

THE STORY OF PHARMACY UNLIMITED

Applying Transformative Faith
Principles to Your Biggest
Challenges

DANNY SKAGGS

Foreword by Jack Sheffield

Prescription for Breakthrough
Applying Transformative Faith Principles to Your Biggest Challenges
Danny Skaggs © 2019

All rights reserved. Use of any part of this publication, whether reproduced, transmitted in any form or by any means, electronic, mechanical, photocopying, recording, or otherwise, or stored in a retrieval system, without the prior consent of the publisher, is an infringement of copyright law and is forbidden.

While the publisher and author have used their best efforts in preparing this book, they make no representations or warranties with respect to the accuracy or completeness of this book and specifically disclaim any implied warranties of merchantability or fitness for a particular purpose. No warranty may be created or extended by sales representatives or written sales materials. The advice and strategies contained herein may not be suitable for your situation. You should consult with a professional where appropriate. Neither the publisher nor the author shall be liable for any loss of profit or any other commercial damages, including but not limited to special, incidental, consequential, or other damages. The stories and interviews in this book are true although the names and identifiable information may have been changed to maintain confidentiality.

The publisher and author shall have neither liability nor responsibility to any person or entity with respect to loss, damage, or injury caused or alleged to be caused directly or indirectly by the information contained in this book. The information presented herein is in no way intended as a substitute for counseling or other professional guidance.

Scripture quotations marked NIV are from the Holy Bible, New International Version® NIV® Copyright © 1973, 1978, 1984, 2011 by Biblica, Inc.™ Used by permission. All rights reserved worldwide.

Scripture quotations marked TPT are from The Passion Translation®. Copyright © 2017 by Broadstreet Publishing® Group, LLC. Used by permission. All rights reserved. Visit ThePassionTranslation.com for more information.

Scripture quotations marked American KJV are from The Study Bible and are not copyrighted. Used by permission. https://study bible.info/version/AKJV. Michael Peter (Stone) Englebrite. Placed on public domain November 8, 1999.

Hardcover ISBN: 978-1-7342244-0-5
eBook ISBN: 978-1-7342244-1-2
Softcover ISBN: 978-1-7342244-2-9

Published by Pharmacy Unlimited

PHARMACY UNLIMITED

Printed in the United States of America

DEDICATION

This book is dedicated to my wife, Kara. With my desire to be in business, recent decisions had caused our income, finances, and retirement funds to become a big mess; yet she never complained. We were near financial ruin with a large debt left as the reminder of the venture into business, yet she never fussed about the circumstances. She stayed in the fight, and in the toughest of the times, she was with me praying, fasting, praising, worshipping, and speaking Scripture into our circumstances. Without her unity in the fight, we would not be able to write this book about our victory. Her unity with me in faith during the fight enabled the victory.

I love you, Kara! Your humble, gentle, patient, tenacious, God-seeking spirit is worthy of distinguishing honor. These small paragraphs of tribute do not adequately honor you, express my gratitude, or express my realization that without your unity and faith in the fight, our outcome would not have been victory. May those who read this appreciate your patient, uncomplaining, faith-speaking support that underlies all the victories recorded in this book. Truly, you helped bring breakthrough, and truly, you are worthy of honor.

CONTENTS

FOREWORD

According to the Small Business Administration (SBA), small businesses account for over half of net job creation in the United States. With over 50 percent of small businesses failing in the first five years of their existence, there is a tremendous need for resources to address this important economic engine.

Many Christians are joining a movement to bring the Kingdom of God and biblical principles into their homes and workplaces. One model of this is called Marketplace Ministry. Christian business leaders and entrepreneurs share wisdom, knowledge, and understanding in how God's salvation through Jesus Christ can impact and strengthen local business communities. Leaders know we spend most of our lives sleeping, and much of our waking time is spent in the workplace doing our jobs. We spend so much energy there on trying to succeed. And it can be the most stressful part of our lives, with so much of our existence hanging in the balance between success and painful failure.

Danny Skaggs is one such leader and entrepreneur who takes on the challenge of gaining true and meaningful advancement in life. He has a great and generous heart for lifting people up, in real life circumstances, into the promise and blessing of discovering their destinies in business settings.

This book informs, inspires, and encourages the Body of Christ (and anyone who will listen) to crush adversity and experience breakthrough in every manner of practical life, not just in business. God is at the center of Danny's story of contending for the kind of riches that only life in Jesus can afford. Anyone who dares to dream the American dream of genuine love of life, authentic prosperity, and lasting peace will appreciate this book.

I know and love this man. He is the real deal! He is funny, intensely thoughtful, insightful, and very caring.

Danny demonstrates that we, too, can become God's masterful workmanship.

Rev. Dr. Jack Sheffield
President, Deep River Ministries
Author of *God's Healing River*[1]

INTRODUCTION

This book tells the amazing story of our survival against all odds, so everyone knows that none of it happened because of our strength or brilliance.

That they may know that this is Your hand; that You, Lord, have done it.
—Psalm 109:27 American KJV

Our story is about breaking through barriers in business; however, the methods we used can be applied in business, athletics, church ministry, education, military, government, law, healthcare, or entertainment.

Barriers appear in any endeavor, and regardless of what they are, the universal laws that broke through our barriers will break through yours.

We applied universal laws created by God, and certainly, the One who created us knows the breakthrough code for any barrier.

The breakthrough codes in this book have been taken from texts that were written centuries ago by the One who created the codes to unlock power, resources, and wisdom beyond our limitations. The codes are authentic and can be used by anyone who believes that their unseen Author has the power to cause them to work, generation after generation after generation. Their Author guarantees the codes. They are universal, so anyone can apply them.

There was a small town where all the residents encountered each other at some point every week of the year. They all knew each other by name and always spoke when they saw each other. Any encounter often developed into a spontaneous conversation. The townspeople noticed that a man named Joe, who incidentally had a stuttering problem, had not been around town for about three weeks. When he reappeared on the town streets after his absence, he encountered his friend Sam. Their discussion follows:

Sam: Hi Joe, where have you been? I haven't seen you for three weeks.

Joe: H-H-Hi S-S-S-Sam, I-I've b-b-been to s-s-speech s-s-s-school.

Sam: That's really good, Joe. What did they teach you?

Joe: Th-Th-They t-t-t-taught m-m-me to s-s-say, How now brown cow? (He said this without stuttering).

Sam: Joe, that's wonderful!

Joe: I-I-It's n-n-n-not t-t-too g-g-g-good. I-I-I-It's s-s-s-s-seldom y-y-you c-c-can w-w-w-work i-i-it i-into th-th-the c-c-c-conversation.

INTRODUCTION

Because it is seldom we can work it into the conversation, we wrote this book to describe the miracles we have witnessed and the power we have discovered that can come from our mouths when we praise God and offer our prayers from the heart. The following chapters memorialize the amazing breakthroughs our family and our business team experienced many times over the years.

This book will teach you universal laws that break any barriers, overcome any hindrance or bondage, and achieve true success and prosperity. This book is a roadmap to freedom. We bless you to find true success, prosperity, and freedom.

God used all the members of Pharmacy Unlimited, as well as every person named in this book. They were His agents and His instruments of blessing; therefore, real names are used, where possible, to honor the people who were such a blessing.

One

BEING IN BUSINESS: A LIFELONG DREAM

I first met Russ Bowman, who was my partner in establishing Pharmacy Unlimited, in 1996 when he walked into my office and applied for a job as a pharmacist. At the time, I was working for Roger Lowe, a lifelong friend and mentor. I was supervising several of his grocery stores, four of which had pharmacies. We needed a pharmacist at that time, so Russ was hired and became an employee of Lowe's Supermarkets.

Russ and I became friends instantly, and we would discuss all kinds of business ideas in the evenings and sometimes during the weekends. Russ was brilliant, creative, and very outgoing. He quickly doubled the sales of the pharmacy he managed, and during the years he managed that pharmacy, he touched the lives of many people in lasting ways.

In August of 1997, I resigned my position at Lowe's and pursued another opportunity that lasted only a few months, and then I went to work for a national pharmacy chain. During this time, Russ and I continued to discuss business ideas. Russ's wife, Christine, a well-educated and accomplished nurse, had contacts with a home health and nursing company that wanted to enlarge their operation to include home infusion pharmacy.

Russ and I were very interested and began talking to the decision-makers at the home health and nursing company. We reached a deal for a 50-50 partnership, with Russ and I owning 50 percent of the new pharmacy and the nursing company owning 50 percent. It was to be a "closed-door" pharmacy, which meant it was not open to the public. Pharmacy Unlimited is still not open to the public, to this day.

In the partnership agreement, the nursing company would furnish office space, inventory, support personnel, and any capital for equipment and other necessary things. Russ had some money, but I had no money with which to start a business, so this idea was attractive. An agreement was signed, and we opened for business on January 2, 1999.

For the next two years, the home infusion concept did not do as well as either partner had hoped. On December 10, 2000, the CEO of the home health and nursing company notified us that they wanted to end the partnership and wanted us out of their building by December 31. The home health company CEO graciously offered to have his two compliance officers assist in transferring all of the licenses and permits of the pharmacy to a new location as a new entity. We accepted his generous offer.

In the new location, our main source of revenue would come from filling nebulizer medications for Part B Medicare patients. In order to prevent a gap in billing to Medicare Part B, the name for Pharmacy Unlimited was not changed, and legal advisors for the home health company decided that Kara Skaggs, my wife, should become the replacement partner for the home health company. The home health company graciously gave us software, computers, an inventory worth $18,000, and supplies.

NEW LOCATION, HUMBLE BEGINNING

On January 2, 2001, Pharmacy Unlimited opened its doors at 206 East 16th Street in Odessa, TX, in a 50-50 partnership with Russ owning 50 percent and Kara and myself owning 50 percent. The pharmacy dispensed nebulizer medications for Part B patients and prescriptions for inmates at a county jail, and was open from 9:00 a.m. until noon, Monday through Friday.

Russ continued to work at Lowe's Supermarkets, and I began working full time as a pharmacist at the inpatient pharmacy of Medical Center Hospital in Odessa. My schedule at the hospital was from 12:30 p.m. until 11:00 p.m.

Russ and I both worked at Pharmacy Unlimited without pay. Russ was our IT person and was responsible for acquiring and maintaining our computers, software, and phone system. We both filled prescriptions and did other necessary things around the pharmacy.

By May 2001, we needed more revenue, so we started filling prescriptions for nursing home patients. We applied for and obtained a Small Business Administration (SBA) loan of about $170,000. We hired Van Bowman, Russ's brother, to market for us, and began working to expand our sales.

Van was quite a marketer and soon he had secured two contracts with Company A. Pharmacy Unlimited filled its first nursing home prescriptions on October 31, 2001. Soon, Van had secured five more contracts with Company B, and we started filling prescriptions for them in January 2002.

Being in business had been a dream for both Russ and me. We thought our business dreams were coming true.

Therefore, when we were successful in obtaining the SBA loan and securing nursing home contracts, we were thrilled. We thought our business dreams were coming true; however, the dreams quickly transitioned to not-so-sweet reality.

A THREAT TO OUR EXISTENCE

By February 1, 2002, it was apparent that the SBA loan was not nearly large enough to purchase inventory, finance accounts receivable, pay salaries, and pay other expenses required to keep the business going. I had always been able to borrow money and expected that the pharmacy's current bank would be glad to loan more. The bank said no. I went to two other banks and asked them to loan money to Pharmacy Unlimited, and all three banks said the business was too leveraged to qualify for any further loans. The banks looked at our finite amount of money, profit, revenue, clients, and huge debt, and said they would not loan us money. They questioned our ability to repay a loan. I do not blame the banks because from their point of view, things were not as financially strong as Russ and I had thought they were.

Our unmet need for money was a warning of disaster. Without additional money to operate, our new business seemed to have a future of maybe a few weeks. My limited vision and reasoning suggested that we "turn out the lights and go home" because circumstances looked impossible. In slightly more than a year after leaving the secure partnership with the home health company, Pharmacy Unlimited was already facing its first threat to existence . . . and it was an overwhelming threat.

In the natural realm, we had nowhere to turn for help.

OVERCOMING OUR FIRST BARRIER

As humans, our abilities to see and reason are finite; therefore, our solutions to problems are finite. All we could see was lack of capital due to unwilling banks. We could see no solution, and we thought that our problems had the potential to bankrupt us.

Did you know that humans are able to see less than 1 percent of the spectrum of light? The human eye is so limited in what it can see that greater than 99 percent of the electromagnetic spectrum (light) is not visible to the human eye. Scientists state that if the human eye could discern the entire spectrum of light, daylight would be less than 1 percent brighter than the night.

In other words, if our vision was not limited, it would be difficult to distinguish the difference between day and night.[2]

If our vision did not have human limitations, it would be difficult to differentiate day from night.

Below is a Scripture written about 3,000 years before the above scientific fact was discovered. It is interesting that scientists discovered the spectrum of light using instruments which did not exist when the Scripture was written. How was this fact known before scientists could discover it?

There is no such thing as darkness with you. The night, to you,
is as bright as the day; there is no difference between the two.
—Psalm 139:12 TPT

Many people have heard that humans use less than 10 percent of their brains. The human brain has developed inventions and innovations that make life much easier than it used to be, but would we have 10 times more inventions and innovations than we do, if we could use all of our brains?

If our brains did not operate with that apparent limitation, would our level of understanding and accomplishment be 10 times greater than it is currently? Or, if we could see more of the spectrum of light and use more than 10 percent of our brains, would we have been able to find a solution in that difficult moment? I don't know.

But at that moment in time, we did not have enough money to continue in business. We had gone to three banks seeking loans, and each of the banks turned us down. It looked like we might not survive as a business. The banks saw our finite amount of money, profit, revenue, clients, and relatively huge debt and concluded that it was not wise to loan us money. If the bankers had been doctors, they would have told us we had a terminal illness and we should get our lives in order.

We were selling prescriptions to help many people, yet we could not dispense a prescription to break through the barrier in our business.

In a simplified overview, we were selling prescriptions to help many people, yet we could not dispense a prescription to break through the barrier in our business.

POWER WALKING

During this same period of time, around February and March of 2002, I began walking around our neighborhood every night after dark. While I was walking, I used what I had been taught in church: I would praise God for about 30 minutes. I used Scripture verses I had learned throughout my life to praise God, as well as just praising Him for who He is and how vast and infinite His creation is. Then for about 30 more minutes, I would speak blessings onto the business. I blessed the business to have surplus growth capital (even though we could not borrow money), best practices in pharmacy, good profitability, no debt, good cash flow, sufficient cash flow to cover growth, and prospective clients reaching out to us. Every night for one hour I walked around the neighborhood praising God and blessing Pharmacy Unlimited. I did this for at least eight years. Any time I drove any distance on highways by myself, I would do the same: praise God and bless Pharmacy Unlimited.

PIVOTAL ADVANTAGE

Pivotal means vitally important and crucial. *Advantage* means superiority of position or condition, benefit, or gain, according to Webster's Seventh New Collegiate Dictionary by G. & C. Merriam Company, Publishers.[3] Therefore, a *pivotal advantage* is a vitally important benefit or a crucially superior position.

The nightly neighborhood power walking gave us a pivotal advantage against the threat to our existence.

Two

IDENTIFYING ENEMIES
AND BREAKING BARRIERS

For approximately 15 years, Kara and I attended a church where Don and Pat Palmer were our pastors. The teaching we received from them advanced our knowledge of the Kingdom of God and God's principles. I called Pastor Don and told him Pharmacy Unlimited was in trouble financially and we must urgently have help from God in order to survive. Toward the end of February 2002, Don arranged for Kara and me to meet with him, Pat, and two other couples on a Tuesday night at Life Unlimited Church. The group prayed for our business and for us, for 30 minutes to an hour. One lady in the group suggested we find a Scripture that spoke to us, repeat it often, and make it a foundational practice for staying in business and getting the help we needed from God. Below is the Scripture I chose:

I will call upon the Lord who is worthy to be praised: so shall I be saved from my enemies. —*Psalm 18:3 American KJV*

Our challenges (or current "enemies") were a lack of cash flow and an inability to borrow money from any bank. In reflection, we could have rephrased the Scripture to read, "I will call upon the Lord who is worthy to be praised: so shall I be saved from lack of cash flow and inability to borrow money from any bank." Unfortunately,

I was not at peace enough at the time to confess it that way, but I would surely say it that way now. Certainly, God knew what we needed and worked on our behalf, even if we did not identify our enemies as lack of cash flow and inability to borrow money when we quoted that Scripture.

About two weeks passed and no form of financial help or breakthrough had appeared, after praying with the three other couples at church. Things looked much worse at this point, though Russ put another $10,000 of his money into the business. I was beginning to agree with the banks, and I began meeting with our employees individually. I told them that it looked like the business was going to fail and they might want to find another job.

Russ and I agreed that he needed to tell Van we could no longer afford to pay him. Van left our employment, but that was no fix for our cash flow problems.

Calling each employee off to the side and telling them we were probably going to fail as a business was one of the most humbling things I have ever done. Telling each person individually, face to face, made me recognize the pride I had carried for my entire life. It was so uncomfortable that I had to gather the courage to talk to each person.

DOES GOD DO MIRACLES TODAY?

We needed more capital. Banks, which are the standard source of capital, said no to our request; this thrust us into a desperate position. We needed a miracle to improve our circumstances, so we turned to the Bible for encouragement and instruction because it has many stories of miracles. The Creation Studies Institute says that 233 miracles are recorded in both the Old and New Testaments. You can find this information on their website.[4] Furthermore, some people who wrote the books of the Bible stated that not all of the miracles God performed were written in the Bible. The Bible looked like a good source of inspiration for us.

The stories in the Bible are about people in impossible places who were delivered from those places by God. Since many of those Bible stories involve Jewish prophets, priests, and kings, it is probably common to think you need to be Jewish, a prophet, priest, or king for God to perform a miracle on your behalf. In addition, it is probably common to think that unless you are on a mission assigned to you by God, He will not perform a miracle on your behalf. Some theologians believe that God no longer does miracles in modern times.

Those thoughts and beliefs created barriers for us as we considered asking God for a miracle; therefore, we had to get past two big questions: 1) Does God still do miracles today? And 2) Will God do a miracle for us?

We were not looking for opinions from people or church doctrines for our answers; we were looking for what God said in His Word about doing miracles in our present day.

Kara and I were not born Jewish; we are Gentiles (the rest of the world), but Gentiles are included in God's plans. The Bible was given to the world through the nation of Israel, and Israelites are referred to as God's chosen people. The Bible reveals that God intended for the entire world to receive His message as shown by the following Scriptures. A good portion of the New Testament states it is God's will for the Gospel to be taken to Gentiles (all nations). Please consider the following Scriptures:

First of all, the Jews have been entrusted with the very words of God.
—Romans 3:2 NIV

25

For I am not ashamed of the gospel, because it is the power of
God that brings salvation to everyone who believes:
first to the Jew, then to the Gentile.
—Romans 1:6 NIV

Or is God the God of Jews only? Is he not the God of Gentiles too?
Yes, of Gentiles too, since there is only one God, who will justify the
circumcised by faith and the uncircumcised through that same faith.
—Romans 3:29 NIV

The Bible stories of Rahab and Ruth establish a precedent that God will perform miracles for people who are not Jewish, prophets, priests, or kings. Rahab and Ruth were foreigners (Gentiles). One was a prostitute and the other was a young widow born in a country that God had cursed. They were both very ordinary people living in circumstances that offered no hope; yet their circumstances were miraculously changed by what they spoke. The words these two women spoke brought them into the lineage of King David and King Jesus.

Salmon the father of Boaz, whose mother was **Rahab***, Boaz the father*
of Obed, whose mother was **Ruth***, Obed the father of Jesse,*
and Jesse the father of King David.
—Matthew 1:5-6 NIV

When a foreigner resides among you in your land, do not mistreat them.
—Leviticus 19:33 NIV

You will find the story of Rahab in Joshua 2:1-21 and Joshua 6:17. You will find the story of Ruth in the book of Ruth in the Old Testament.

We were desperate and we believed God would perform a miracle for us. If the business failed, we would be in a lot of debt. Our desperations kept us focused on power walking and prayer.

OUR FIRST MIRACLE

On a Friday morning in March 2002, I had decided to notify our clients that Pharmacy Unlimited was going to close, and that they would need to find another pharmacy. Just as I was finishing the thoughts of that plan, Bob Avary, a friend, called and asked what was going on. I told him. Bob invited me to lunch to hear more about my challenges. By the end of that day, Bob had arranged that he and his sister would loan $100,000 to Pharmacy Unlimited. Bob's confidence in putting that much money into Pharmacy Unlimited gave me confidence to borrow $80,000 from my mother.

From that one phone call, Pharmacy Unlimited suddenly had operational money that did not come from banks. We were delivered from the huge threat that could have closed our doors.

About this time, Russ inherited a beautiful waterfront property on Lake LBJ (Lake Lyndon B. Johnson) and it was a dream come true for him. Russ wanted to sell out of Pharmacy Unlimited and move to his newly acquired lakefront property. It was a choice that either one of us would have taken over grinding things out in a struggling business. Russ and I both enjoyed fishing and we had fished before at the newly inherited property. I would have done the exact same thing if I had been in his shoes.

We needed to buy out Russ's interest in the company. Kara and I talked to Bill Elms, a well-respected CPA and the primary partner of the CPA firm that employed Kara, about appraising the value of 50 percent of Pharmacy Unlimited.

Bill set the value of Russ's half at about $45,000. Bob Avary drew up a simple buyout agreement, consisting of terms for a $1,000 cash down payment and 60 monthly payments for the balance. The first payment was due in October 2002.

The agreement for the five-year buyout of Russ's half of the business was signed in the first week of May 2002. Russ did not know how much I was praying we would make those 60 payments and make them on time.

Much of Scripture promises God's willingness to help people who find themselves in impossible circumstances. Scripture is historic and prophetic in nature, telling both what God has done in the past and what He will do in the future for the nation of Israel, the world, and anyone who trusts Him.

Kara and I wholeheartedly accepted the notion that Scripture's promises are without restrictions to time, nationality, dispensation, denomination, or other reasoning of finite minds. Though our circumstances were different, Kara and I were as desperate as Rahab and Ruth, so we rejected the notion that God does not perform miracles today.

We believed we had our answers: God still does miracles today and He would do miracles for us.

WHAT YOU BELIEVE (WHAT YOU ACT ON) IS CRITICAL

Joe Amaral, in his book *Understanding Jesus: Cultural Insights into the Words and Deeds of Christ,*[5] describes faith: "Faith is the very thing that drives us to continue when our circumstances tell us differently. Faith is what gives us hope to persevere against all odds. It is at the core of who we are as followers of Christ." Faith in God was the only reason we kept going.

INSPIRATION FROM A BARRIER-BREAKER

Roger Bannister breaking the barrier of a four-minute mile has always been a fascinating story to me because he believed he could break a barrier that many thought impossible. Claire Nana, LMFT, wrote a paragraph that best describes this in her May 2017 article titled "The Four Minute Mile, the Two Hour Marathon, and the Danger of Glass Ceilings":[6]

> "Before Roger Bannister broke the four-minute mile on May 6th, 1954, on Iffley Road Track in Oxford, physiologists, doctors, and athletes themselves had contended that running a mile in under four minutes wasn't only impossible, it might actually lead to death. The human body simply wasn't equipped to accomplish such a feat, they said. On a deeper level the message was clear: there are certain limits about ourselves that must be observed, certain limits that we simply can't surpass. **Bannister had a different belief**. At the time, himself studying to be a physician, Bannister didn't just think that the human body could, in fact, run a mile in under four minutes, but that *he* was the one to do it. And after he broke the record that day in Oxford, running an amazing 3 minutes, 59.4 seconds, just 46 days later, the record was broken again."

This story inspires me because Roger Bannister successfully broke through a barrier **because he believed he could**. After he broke the barrier, many others were able to break through the same barrier, and his world record for running the mile lasted only 46 days. Until Roger Bannister broke the four-minute barrier, prevailing thought had maintained the barrier upon a faulty premise. After the premise was proven faulty, the barrier no longer existed. So, if we are looking at circumstances with a faulty premise, are we creating a barrier that should not be there?

The fascinating thing about barriers is that after a barrier is broken, it is easier for others to break through the same barrier. In his article on Smithsonian.com titled "Five Things to Know About Roger Bannister, the First Person to Break the 4-Minute Mile," Jason Daley reflected on this by saying, "Kevin J. Delaney at *Quartz* reports that Bannister's records did not live much past the summer of 1954.[7] Since then, 500 American men alone have broken the 4-minute mark, including 21 who have done so since the beginning of this year."

Three

SOMETHING MORE VALUABLE THAN GOLD

What we actually needed in our business was not available in banks, but it took us some time to realize this.

There was once a rich man who had a lot of gold. He was very proud of his riches. This man prayed all the time and was very close to the Lord. One night as he was praying, he sensed that he would be dying soon. In his prayer, he asked the Lord for permission to bring to Heaven one item very important to him. In His great love and wisdom, the Lord responded that earthly things are not allowed into Heaven, but because they had been so close in prayer, He would make an exception. Many stories and jokes depict St. Peter managing the pearly gates of Heaven, so we will use that picture here. Therefore, the story goes that the rich man died and arrived at the pearly gate of Heaven with a suitcase full of gold. His conversation with St. Peter follows:

St. Peter: Sir, you cannot bring that suitcase into Heaven.

Rich man: The Lord has given me permission to bring my suitcase into Heaven. Why don't you check with Him?

St. Peter: I am not sure about that, but I will check. I'll be gone a short while. Wait here.

St. Peter left to inquire of the Lord, and then returned.

St. Peter: Sir, the Lord approved you bringing your suitcase into Heaven. He asked me to inspect its contents before you enter.

St. Peter opened the man's suitcase and then spoke to the man.

St. Peter: Sir, if you could bring anything into Heaven, why would you bring pavement?

A SUPERIOR VALUE SYSTEM

The joke about taking gold to Heaven illustrates the difference in the value systems of the two realms: the natural realm versus the heavenly realm. What is precious, rare, and locked in vaults in the natural realm is so common in the heavenly realm that it is laid on streets to walk upon. If the prized standard of wealth in the natural realm is walked upon in the heavenly realm, then what is of greatest worth in Heaven? Is it possible that what is of greatest worth in the heavenly realm is also of greater worth than gold in the natural realm?

The illustration of gold's value in the natural versus the heavenly realms suggests a provocative contrast in value. What is rare and valuable on earth is so common in Heaven that it is used as a construction material. Identifying what is at the apex of value in Heaven will certainly be of greatest value on earth, even if we do not have the wisdom to regard it as such. These Scriptures give us a hint:

> *. . . for You have magnified Your word above all Your name.*
> *—Psalm 138:2b American KJV*

> *. . . for You have so exalted Your solemn decree that it surpasses Your fame.*
> *—Psalm 138:2b NIV*

. . . for the promises of Your word and the fame of Your name have been magnified above all else! —Psalm 138:2b TPT

In Heaven, God's name and His Word are exalted above all else.

God's name and His Word are the apex of value in Heaven.

It is worth establishing in our thought processes that everything in the natural realm is subordinate to the governance of the heavenly realm. What is below is governed by what is above. The heavenly realm is eternal . . . everlasting. The natural realm is temporal . . . it is aging and not everlasting.

So, said differently, the everlasting governs the temporal. Regardless of our lack of discernment and understanding, what is of great worth, importance, and power in the heavenly, eternal realm has the same great worth, importance, and power in the natural, temporal realm. As we established in the last paragraph, God's Word and His name have governance in the natural realm.

So shall my word be that goes forth out of my mouth: it shall not return unto me void, but it shall accomplish that which I please, and it shall prosper in the thing whereto I sent it.
—Isaiah 55:11 American KJV

So is my word that goes forth out of my mouth: it will not return to me empty, but will accomplish what I desire and achieve the purpose for which I sent it. —Isaiah 55:11 NIV

Proverbs 8:10-11 reveals that the things we secure in vaults such as gold, silver, and jewels are not the most valuable things. These two verses reveal the existence of something far more valuable than the money we were not able to borrow.

My wise correction is more valuable than silver or gold. The finest gold is nothing compared to the revelation-knowledge I can impart. Wisdom is so priceless that it exceeds the value of any jewel. Nothing you can wish for can equal her. —Proverbs 8:10-11 TPT

Since the natural realm is subordinate to the heavenly realm, knowing what has the highest worth in Heaven is a **pivotal advantage** in circumstances here on earth.

DEVASTATING NEWS

The second week of May 2002, one week after committing to buy out Russ, I learned that our largest customer, Company B, had filed Chapter 11 bankruptcy. When I learned this, I was in Pampa, Texas, at one of Company B's nursing homes, and as I drove home from Pampa, it took me an hour or better to recover from my stunned state. Our biggest account owed us money and they had filed for bankruptcy. We were barely making it, and we had just committed to buying Russ Bowman's half of the pharmacy. It was obvious that God's power was the only solution to this new threat to Pharmacy Unlimited. As best I could, I praised God for His power over all circumstances.

Upon arriving home, I learned that Company B owed Pharmacy Unlimited about $60,000. Since there was no immediate prospect of that being paid, I contacted our bank and told them that I needed $50,000 and that we would repay the loan and interest monthly over the next 12 months. The bank agreed to the loan and terms rather than taking possession of Pharmacy Unlimited.

At this time, I thought Russ Bowman was definitely smarter than I was. He had sold his interest in our partnership before we got the news of Company B filing bankruptcy. Russ was free of the stress of the business, and not only was I still dealing with it, but we had just learned of another devastating threat to our existence. With this news, things were so hopeless financially that I'm surprised Kara did not issue an ultimatum that we abandon this failing project and get free from the overwhelming circumstances; yet, instead of an ultimatum, she joined me in prayer, worked for no pay, and believed that we would make it.

In the days, weeks, and months ahead, Kara and I did a lot of praying. Even with the $50,000 loan, finances were tight. I had left full-time employment at the hospital in November 2002, and I was not being paid a salary for my full-time work at Pharmacy Unlimited. When I could, I did relief pharmacist work in the evenings or on Saturdays to supplement income. Kara and I were living on her salary from the accounting firm that employed her, and when our living expenses exceeded her salary each month, we added the balance to our credit card debt.

During this time, we paid at least two payrolls for our entire staff by borrowing the money from our personal credit cards. On three separate occasions, I had to call our drug wholesaler (the company selling us the medications we dispensed) to tell them we could only make a partial payment on the statement that was due twice a month. The balance of the partial payment was always paid within a week, and the wholesaler always charged the pharmacy a substantial late fee.

I kept saying, "It is just money." I said that so often it became a habit, and that habit dwarfed barriers into a better perspective. In spite of the threats such as reluctant banks and client bankruptcies, Kara and I prayed and trusted God to supply the money we needed to pay the bills and remain solvent. God never let us down.

We kept going this way, and we added three very good clients in June, July, and October of 2002, and by October 2002, we added a part-time pharmacist to the pharmacy staff. By December 2002, the business was growing more, the part-time pharmacist became full time, and bills and invoices were being paid on time.

Kara and I were growing in our faith in God and in our personal relationships with God. Said differently, Kara and I were beginning to really "know God" instead of only "knowing about God." The financial hardships and threats to Pharmacy Unlimited were the ways by which Kara and I really got to know God, His Word, and the truth, power, stability, permanency, protection, hope, and deliverance that lie hidden like treasure in God's Word . . . waiting for discovery by any person who will believe and seek.

I continued to walk at night, using verses out of Scripture to praise God for who He is and how He watches over His Word spoken out of our mouths. My pattern was always the same: 30 minutes praising God out of Scripture and 30 minutes speaking blessings onto Pharmacy Unlimited.

It is important to remind you that banks would not loan us money. Our own bank only loaned us $50,000 so they would not have to assume the pharmacy. It is important to remind you that I blessed Pharmacy Unlimited every night to have more growth capital than we needed.

Pharmacy Unlimited's driver drove about 350 miles daily to deliver meds to our clients, and Bob Avary offered the use of a 1987 vehicle he owned at no charge. To avoid adding cost to our operation, we decided to use it for deliveries and found that the vehicle's gas mileage was poor. The vehicle's operating expenses were also expensive and after two months, we bought a new F-150 two-door pickup that would carry no more than three passengers. The pickup's fuel savings compared to the 1987 vehicle saved enough to make its monthly payment.

A MIRACLE BREAKTHROUGH

In August 2003, two ladies from a bank we had never visited during our earlier funding efforts walked into Pharmacy Unlimited and stated that they were looking for new business. In other words, they said, "We're here to loan you money." We needed a bank that believed in us as a business, so Kara began working with the two ladies on transferring to their bank.

The president of their bank came by to talk to us and explained how they arrived at a loan amount. Believe it or not, that formula produced the amount of money we needed for future growth. They were eager to help us in other areas that benefitted us as well. Our relationship with our new bank began and we had $250,000 available to borrow. It seemed as if reproach had been removed from us.

Within 18 months of our beginning to bless our business with more growth capital than we needed, representatives from a bank walked into our business looking for the opportunity to loan us money. They were so eager to help us that they bought a loan we had with Ford Motor Credit and moved it to their bank at a lesser rate of interest. That loan was for the pickup we purchased.

The nightly power walks continued. The spoken blessings of growth capital, profitability, being a best-practices leader, freedom from debt, growth funding cash flow, and prospective clients attracted to Pharmacy Unlimited continued. Certainly, praises to God continued. Our faith in speaking over our circumstances was certainly encouraged by our new bank's attitude toward us.

MORE MIRACLE BREAKTHROUGHS

In January 2004, Kara and I were in Dallas visiting our daughter and her husband on a Saturday morning when Kara's cell phone rang. Kara's mother and father wanted to "loan" us $100,000. Kara and I had not asked for the "loan" nor mentioned any need for money to them. Very unexpectedly and not influenced by any information from us, Kara's mother and father were offering us $100,000. This money would be growth capital for Pharmacy Unlimited.

A few months later, Kara's mother and father called again, and added another $50,000 to the "loan," making the total they had "loaned" us $150,000. Pharmacy Unlimited had more growth capital than we needed, and Kara and I grew in faith. As you can imagine, we were getting to know God through the power of His Word and His help in our circumstances. We later learned that Kara's parents were "loaning" the same amount of money to their two sons and their gift was not motivated by any knowledge of our circumstances.

Can you believe it? We now had more growth capital than we needed, exactly as the blessings were spoken over Pharmacy Unlimited. What we spoke over our circumstances had come true! Even more amazing was the realization that the money came to us without any effort on our part to ask for it.

OUR ANSWERS CAME OUT OF OUR MOUTHS

Here is my conclusion from the above experiences: Things that look like failures are not failures unless you begin calling them that. Things that look like failures can become successes if you call them that. The tongue has power to bring death . . . or life . . . depending on what you consistently say.

By your spoken words bringing life into people or circumstances, an apparent failure becomes transformed and redeemed through God's power, which has been mysteriously placed by Him into His Word and our tongues speaking His Word. Our mistake is to think that this process always happens instantly.

Here is a Scripture from two Bible translations to establish my above statements:

Death and life are in the power of the tongue: and they that love it shall eat the fruit thereof. —Proverbs 18:21 American KJV

The tongue has the power of life and death, and those who love it will eat its fruit. —Proverbs 18:21 NIV

It is amazing for me to reflect on our trials and realize that our answers and our help came out of our mouths . . . our mouths speaking praises to God and blessings. The answers and help for our problems came out of our mouths! **We didn't say how things looked; instead we spoke how we wanted things to look.**

The power in the promises of God's Word spoken out of our mouths changed things.

We can create solutions or problems with our mouths. The Scriptures in Proverbs offer encouragement as well as warning about what comes out of our mouths.

Below is a Scripture with a warning.

You are snared with the words of your mouth; you are taken with the words of your mouth. —Proverbs 6:2 American KJV

IN SUMMARY

Though lack of growth capital and cash flow were barriers, we broke through those barriers by using something more valuable than money . . . more valuable than gold. What we used was not found locked in bank vaults. By declining to loan us money, the banks enabled us to discover something more valuable than money.

Our apparent need was money; our true need was all the resources from Heaven.

Regardless of how ominous and foreboding the barrier in your path is, it is easily eliminated by the infinite power of God released when the promises of His Word are spoken against that barrier. God's Word, principles, and laws will break through any earthly barrier because the heavenly rules over the earthly.

Four

IS THIS PRESCRIPTION FOR BREAKTHROUGH WORKING?

Business moved along without threat from 2004 until the end of 2006. At the end of 2006 and the beginning of 2007, Pharmacy Unlimited began losing clients for various reasons, one at a time over a few months. One client went bankrupt, another went to another long-term care pharmacy, and others had unforeseen issues. We were not alarmed because we were marketing and expecting new clients to come onto our service.

For about a year, we had been looking for a new location for the pharmacy because we had outgrown the space we were leasing. Kara felt drawn to one particular building, so we had been praying about buying that building for nearly a year. During the time we were praying, another buyer made an offer to buy that building. Now we had another buyer in line ahead of us to purchase the building.

Nonetheless, Kara intuitively felt that we would be buying the building, and one night in February 2007 she was inspired to walk around the building seven times while praying. We went together and prayed as we walked around the building. We continued to pray for guidance regarding the purchase of the building, knowing that someone else might buy it.

During the first week of April 2007, our marketer for the past two and a half years, who we will refer to as Gary, resigned and went to work for our largest client, which we call Company 28, because it was 28 percent of our business. Gary's father-in-law, who had also worked for us, was working for a competitor pharmacy.

We were aware that the father-in-law was trying to take business away from us, so we did damage control the best we knew how. We knew it was possible that Gary and his father-in-law would team up at Company 28, who had just hired Gary. Through these developments, the stage was being set for us to see firsthand another great breakthrough from God.

During the month of June, the other interested party changed their mind about buying the building and withdrew their offer. A date was set for Kara and me to sign the purchase papers in our attorney's office. Incidentally, the building we were buying had a national company as tenant and there were three years left on their lease contract, even though the tenant had vacated the building. Since the tenant was still paying the lease each month, we calculated that the lease payments would actually pay the mortgage on the building. Even if we decided not to move immediately, it looked like a great deal. July 12, 2007, 11:00 a.m. was set as the closing on the purchase of the building.

IT LOOKS LIKE POWER WALKING IS NOT WORKING

On the morning of July 12, 2007, at about 10:00 a.m., a letter from Company 28 was delivered with the mail. The letter was less than 60 days' notice that Company 28, who was still the largest client of Pharmacy Unlimited, was moving their business to another pharmacy. We were being fired (and yes, it was the client that Gary had gone to work for in April).

We had one hour until we were supposed to sign the papers to buy a building, and we had just received notice that we were going to lose more than a quarter of our business, bringing the total business loss to date to an overwhelming 48 percent. We knew we were facing a monstrous threat to the existence of our business and we were stunned.

Kara and I placed our hands on the letter of bad news and began to pray. We called the letter a lie. Kara even wrote across the letter, "This is a lie." The letter is still in our files. We asked the Lord to tell us whether or not to buy the building, and did not hear a word from the Lord.

We prayed a great deal in that hour before our appointment in the attorney's office. We calculated that the current lease on the building would cover the cost of the building for three years. We calculated that business should turn around during that time, and since we needed more operating space anyway, we would go ahead with purchasing the building. We went to that closing and bought the building.

At that time, our son Nathan and his wife, Alana, were living with us in our home, before they moved to Amarillo so Nathan could begin pharmacy school; therefore, Nathan and Alana were in the midst of those stressful months with us. They participated in the prayers and the fasting, along with many of the employees of Pharmacy Unlimited who were faithful to pray and fast with us. Anytime people are in a threatening circumstance, the prayers of other people are enormously comforting. All of the people who prayed with us were a tremendous comfort and support.

A DEFINING MOMENT

On a Sunday afternoon, July 22, 2007, I went into the newly purchased building and made a declaration inspired by Job 22:28:

You shall also decree a thing, and it shall be established unto you:
and the light shall shine upon your ways.
—Job 22:28 American KJV

My declaration: "I declare that Pharmacy Unlimited will occupy this building by July 31, 2008." When I made that declaration, nothing looked good for Pharmacy Unlimited. The pharmacy had lost 48 percent of its business and by September 2007, the pharmacy began losing money because of the loss of Company 28's business.

The reality of the loss of 48 percent of our business was like a mountain blocking our path and was very stressful. Once again, a huge threat to our existence had appeared.

The declaration was spoken aloud into the building because of an inner prompting. After I spoke the declaration, things happened in the spiritual realm on our behalf even though nothing was visible. In retrospect, it is easy to see that God began arranging for new clients, the return of former clients, a construction company for remodel of the newly purchased building, and an early buyout of the tenant's lease. In retrospect, though invisible to our eyes at the time, light was shining upon our challenges and decisions.

GREATEST PRESSURE BEFORE BREAKTHROUGH

One afternoon, very near the end of July 2007, things looked so discouraging. The stress weighed heavily on me. I went home for a while and was in the master bathroom of our home, pacing the floor, praising God, and praying when my cell phone rang. A lady asked for David and, annoyed, I said, "This isn't David." The lady then asked if she was speaking to Pharmacy Unlimited. The call was from a nursing home administrator in San Antonio, and she was calling to let me know she was ready for Pharmacy Unlimited to start serving her large nursing home.

I had been in San Antonio in May 2007 and had gone by her nursing home to see her. At that time, she did not have time to talk to me. Following her call to me in July, this nursing home became our largest single account when we began serving them in October 2007.

Additionally, on Sunday, July 29, 2007, Dr. John Benefiel spoke at Life Unlimited Church in Odessa and mentioned that the ancient god of Canaan, Phoenicia, and Mesopotamia was Baal, and Baal had become a principality over America.

He taught us about two important spiritual instruments that we could use. One was a Decree of Divorce from Baal (Baal is mentioned many times as a false god in the Bible), and the other instrument was a Petitioner's Original Request to present in the Highest Court in the Universe . . . the Court of Heaven. They are listed below.

Dr. Benefiel led Life Unlimited Church in divorcing Baal, but the Baal Divorce Decree presented here was transcribed from a television program when Dr. Benefiel was a guest on Sid Roth's "It's Supernatural."

The Petitioner's Original Request was given to us as a handout at the church service in Odessa; however, you can find both of these in Dr. John Benefiel's book *Binding the Strongman Over America.*[8]

Dr. Benefiel mentioned that Baal has crept into American life, and that he is assigned to hold back the promises of God and to control the earth and its wealth. As written in Dr. Benefiel's book, "Baal is the principality behind pornography and every kind of sexual sin. Baal is the principality behind all human sacrifice, whether in the form of satanic worship or abortion." The false god Baal influences so many things in America that Dr. Benefiel recommended we corporately divorce Baal in our church. Certainly, we did not want the promises of God restrained, so we followed his recommendation.

I felt that God had encouraged me to focus our marketing efforts in Company 28's headquarter city. In addition to Company 28, we had acquired other clients in that city through our God-directed marketing. I felt that He had given to us the accounts we gained, and if He gave us the clients, He would *not* take them away from us.

BAAL DIVORCE DECREE

Plainly put, Company 28 had been stolen from us, and we needed an intervention; therefore, the Petitioner's Original Request seemed like the right instrument to use in getting that business back. We took the Scripture references listed by Dr. Benefiel and adopted their wording to our circumstances:

> Dear Lord Jesus, I turn from my wicked ways. I want to follow you, Lord Jesus. I ask You to grant me a divorce from the principality of Baal, the ruler of the demons. I want nothing to do with this evil principality. I want You and You alone, Lord Jesus, so I declare that I am divorced from Baal and married to the Lord Jesus Christ now and always. Amen.

PETITIONER'S ORIGINAL REQUEST

Based on Ephesians 6:17-18:

This petition is being brought to God because of His Word. It is being brought to the Highest Court of the Kingdom of God.

Based on Hebrews 4:16:

We come boldly before the Throne of Grace that we may obtain mercy and find grace in time of need.

Based on John 2:1-2:

I am represented by Jesus Christ, my Advocate. There has been a change of representation by counsel and Satan no longer represents me because he is not my lord or lawyer any longer.

Based on Psalm 100:4:

I am thankful that I can petition this court, for God has done great things for me. My account has been identified by the written Word, and again I want to give thanks. All relief for petitioners was granted in full.

Based on Psalm 116:1-2:

The basis for grant of relief in contract is established by the Old Covenant with Abraham, because God could swear by no greater, He swore by Himself. But, I have a better covenant established upon better promises. I became an heir, through my Agent, Jesus, when He sealed it by His blood for a new covenant.

Based on Psalm 89:14:

This petition is being brought to the Court of the Most High God for justice. Justice and judgment are the habitation of Your throne. Mercy and Truth shall go before Your face. So, Father, we ask You for justice in our behalf.

Based on Isaiah 9:7:

There is no end to Jesus' government and peace. His Kingdom is established and is upheld with justice and with righteousness for evermore. The zeal of the Lord of Hosts will perform this, and we petition You, Lord of Hosts, to perform this in our behalf.

Based on II Chronicles 20:7:

Lord God, did You not give us these accounts? Did You not tell us to go to _____ (name of city in which the accounts were headquartered)?

Based on II Chronicles 20:9:

Because the thief is coming upon us, we stand before You and cry to You in our affliction and You will hear us and save us according to Your Word.

Therefore, I have every right to be here and have the relief sought, and You, God, have the authority to issue a decree in this matter.

I request to be granted the following specific requests for relief, and hereby petition You to do the following:

- Reverse the decision to award the nursing homes to a competitor pharmacy because You gave the _____ (name of city) territory to us.

- Command the blessing upon us in the territory that You gave us. (Deuteronomy 28:8)

- Restrain Satan from destroying us and our business since You have nurtured and preserved and saved Pharmacy Unlimited as a business dedicated to You and to marketplace ministry on Your behalf. (Deuteronomy 28:8-14)

- Rebuke the devourer for our sakes, so that he does not destroy the fruits of our ground, which You have given us. We have brought all the tithes into the storehouse according to Your command. (Malachi 3:8)

- Force Satan to stop resisting our efforts of growth and prosperity. (Malachi 3:8)

- Turn the evil that has been done to us to good regarding this account that is 28 percent of our business. (Romans 8:28)

- Look on the iniquity done to us and recompense us with good. (II Samuel 16:12)

- Command the blessings of Abraham to come upon us in Christ Jesus that we might receive the promise of the Spirit through faith. (Galatians 3:4)

- Rescue us because we do not repay evil, but we wait expectantly for You, Lord, to rescue us. (Proverbs 20:22)

- Look down from Your holy habitation and bless Your people of Pharmacy Unlimited, and restore the accounts You have given us. (Deuteronomy 26:15)

- Keep any weapon that is formed against us from prospering and show the tongues that have risen in judgment against us to be in the wrong. (Isaiah 54:17)

- Give us triumph over opposition because this is our heritage as servants of the Lord, and because this is the vindication which we obtain from the Lord as our justification. (Isaiah 54:17)

- Make Satan restore sevenfold since Your Word states that if a thief be found he shall restore sevenfold.

Since Satan has been found stealing the accounts You have given us, we ask that he be required by Your command to repay us sevenfold. (Proverbs 6:30-31)

This is the petitioner's prayer: that You, the Highest Authority in the universe, grant a summary judgment in this matter. For Satan has come as a thief to steal, kill, and to destroy, but Your promise to me was in Your Word and by Your Spirit, which You gave me. (John 10:10 and Psalm 119:170)

I cast all of my care on You, **for I know You have heard me, and I have it.** (Psalm 4:6-8)

So, therefore, it is ordered, adjudged, and decreed that the petitioner receive that relief sought in this petition immediately, according to Mark 11:23-24 and I John 5:14-15.

Be it further ordered, adjudged, and decreed that the agents of God implement such findings immediately pursuant to the Word. In other words, Holy Spirit and angels do God's Word. **Again, let me say thank You for all You have done and are now doing.** I know You shall continue to bless all who seek and serve You. (Psalm 103:20)

Dated this 2nd Day of August 2007

Petitioners:

Signed: _____

Signed: _____

Answered this the _____ Day of _____, 20__

Filling out the Petitioner's Original Request took a few days, but we filled it out, read it aloud in prayer, signed and dated it, and filed it in our files. As you can see above, the Petition was presented, signed, and entered in Heaven's Court on August 2, 2007.

Knowing that the Court of Heaven has authority over all courts on earth and even over earthly circumstances is vitally important. Knowing that you can take a matter before the Court of Heaven and knowing that you have a lawyer in the Court of Heaven who will defend you is yet **another pivotal advantage.**

OPPORTUNITY OPPOSITE OF REASON

In August 2007, our church had an immediate need for several new air conditioners, which looked impossible with their current finances. Our business was about to have a financial need that looked impossible if Company 28's account went away. Looking back, the simultaneous timing of the financial need at our church and the financial need in our business was more than coincidental. It was an opportunity for us to bring God's power into our financial need in our business. The amount required to cover the air conditioners needed at church would have bought a small house in Odessa's economy at the time; yet Kara and I were inspired by the Scripture below to give an offering that would pay for the church's air conditioning need.

Give, and it will be given to you. A good measure, pressed down, shaken together and running over, will be poured into your lap. For with the measure you use, it will be measured to you.
—Luke 6:38 NIV

PRESCRIPTION FOR BREAKTHROUGH

Give generously and generous gifts will be given back to you, shaken down to make room for more. Abundant gifts will pour out upon you with such an overflowing measure that it will run over the top! Your measurement of generosity becomes the measurement of your return.
—*Luke 6:38 TPT*

We did not have excess money in the bank, and we were giving money out of a business that was about to start losing money. We were giving out of an impossible financial need in our business entity to alleviate the impossible financial need of another entity. In view of our circumstances, we felt we were using a very large "measure."

Though it appeared that Pharmacy Unlimited could not afford to give that much money, the measure we used in giving guaranteed a return to us using a like measure. Our measure covered all of the church's need, so the measure used to return to us would cover all of our need. We were giving our measure for the promised measure that would come out of God's realm into our circumstances.

God sees all things. God responds to faith in Him and His Word. Kara and I were establishing with our gift that our threatening circumstances were not more powerful than our belief in God's Word. In addition, even though we had just made a large gift to the church, we were not intimidated by tight finances to stop regular tithing and giving.

The way Luke 6:38 is worded reveals that it is a principle or law. This Scripture says that giving will always be returned to you. The only condition influencing how this principle or law works is the measure the giver uses in giving. If you use a wheelbarrow to measure how much you give, a wheelbarrow will be used to measure how much comes back to you; if you use a teaspoon to measure how much you give, a teaspoonful will come back to you. The use of a generous measure will cause much more to come back to you than the worth of your gift.

How this law works is concealed in a mystery: the law does not work by the value of the gift; instead, the law works by the generosity of the giver.

The most famous illustration of how your measure is evaluated is found in Luke 21:1-4, where a widow gives two little copper coins into the Temple treasury. Jesus commented that it was all she had, so she had given more than others who gave silver or gold coins.

As Jesus looked up, He saw the rich putting their gifts into the temple treasury. He also saw a poor widow put in two very small copper coins. "Truly I tell you," he said, "this poor widow has put in more than all the others. All these people gave their gifts out of their wealth; but she out of her poverty put in all she had to live on."
—Luke 21:1-4 American KJV

(*Knowing that Luke 6:38 applied to the widow in the above Scripture, it would be interesting to see what return followed her giving of the two copper coins.)

IS ANYTHING WE ARE DOING WORKING FROM A SPIRITUAL PERSPECTIVE?

The month of September 2007 arrived and Company 28 moved their business to a competitor pharmacy. Our business level was now at 52 percent of what it had been previously. Before, when business had dropped off, Pharmacy Unlimited downsized expenses by laying off staff. This time, Kara and I sensed that we should not do that; however, every Saturday morning I would sit at my desk and write out a list of employees I should lay off in order to reduce payroll expense.

Every week my list had names on it that I should lay off to reduce payroll, and every week I would throw the list of names I had just written into the trash. In September 2007, with our payroll expenses unchanged from when we had 48 percent more business, Pharmacy Unlimited began losing money.

Company 28 did not answer or return my phone calls or emails; therefore, by mail, I sent a proposal and request to continue serving their account. They did not answer. Weeks passed, and when Christmas approached, I sent the Christmas gifts to their office and facilities like we had done in the past . . . even though they were not talking to me. In March 2008, I sent an email to the owner of the business, requesting a meeting to demonstrate some new software we had available. The owner granted my request, and a meeting was scheduled in April.

BREAKTHROUGH AGAIN

Meanwhile, Alana Skaggs (Nathan's wife), who began marketing for Pharmacy Unlimited in 2007, met with me in San Antonio to call on prospective clients.

Ronnie and Darlene Evans owned a very successful nursing home in Schertz, Texas. Darlene was the administrator and Ronnie was the financial officer. Before he left our employment, Gary and I had been asking this couple for their business for over a year. They had always been very gracious with their time when we came by to ask for their business, but never seemed persuaded to use Pharmacy Unlimited.

This time, Alana and I invited them to dinner. That evening, over dinner, Alana and I had a very good time with Ronnie and Darlene and their high school daughter, Kelsey. After dinner, in the parking lot of the restaurant, Darlene told Alana to schedule a meeting with her staff and convince them to use Pharmacy Unlimited. We began serving that facility in November 2007. Ronnie and Darlene were agents of God. Their decision was encouraging, significant, and an answer to our prayer.

MORE BREAKTHROUGH

In October 2007, we began serving a new client in San Antonio, and that was another encouragement to us. Also in October, Nathan and Alana visited a nursing home in Midland, Texas, and the couple who owned the home immediately gave them the account. Usually, it takes several months for an account to come onto service, but this couple agreed to work with Pharmacy Unlimited in the first meeting. They began using Pharmacy Unlimited in December 2007.

What a year 2007 was. Obviously, with the new accounts, our negative circumstances were reversing and by the end of December, we were in a break-even position. Some people would say that hard work and being in the right place at the right time caused the addition of the new accounts. We were working very hard, marketing and reaching out for new business. We were working very hard, period.

God honors hard work; however, as much as God honors our hard work, I am convinced that He honors in a greater degree His Word spoken out of our mouths.

Five

BEYOND IMAGINATION

In April 2008, I met with the owner of Company 28, who had taken his business to a competitor in September 2007. We had a very amicable meeting, and he announced to me that all of his business would be returning to Pharmacy Unlimited on June 1, 2008. I knew that his business returning to our service was due to God at work through prayer, fasting, praise and worship to God, giving, and speaking God's Word over circumstances. God was also at work through our declaration and petition to the Court of Heaven, because God's Word is always true.

"The Light" had been shining on our ways. Incidentally, all the employees of Pharmacy Unlimited were praying for the pharmacy along with us. Our sons and their wives were praying consistently on our behalf too. We are convinced that God heard all of the prayers. So, when prayer is mentioned anytime in these pages, the picture in my mind is that God heard the voices of many people in prayer. And my belief is that He responded to the voices of many people praying and believing that He hears and answers prayer.

In April 2008, Kara and I thought it was time to begin the move into the new building, not remembering the declaration that I had spoken in the new building in July 2007. We discussed the move with our banker, who advised us to ask the tenant of the building for an early payout on the lease and for a release from the lease contract so that Pharmacy Unlimited could occupy the building. Kara approached the tenant about an early payout and they answered with a desire for prompt action on the early payout. The lease early payout was obtained, and the tenant released the building. As a result, Kara and I had some cash, and we went back to the banker.

We met with our banker over lunch in May 2008 and told him we had done as he had suggested. He had just closed a large deal for the bank that week and showed no interest in helping us finance the move into the building.

During the lunch, I sensed the Lord reminding me of amounts of money from various sources that could be used in addition to the early payout money. As I mentally added up the available money during lunch, I realized it was enough to do the project without help from the bank—if we modified our plans for moving into the building. We politely ended the lunch discussion and went back to the Pharmacy to meet with our staff and plan the move.

Even though the banker's lack of interest appeared to be a barrier to moving forward, God's spiritual principles spoken over our circumstances, months prior to this meeting, provided the resources for us—instead of the banker providing the resources. This happened without debt and on a faster timeline.

Back at the office, we began to look at the calendar with our staff to decide the best weekend to move. As we planned our move into the new building, I still failed to remember the declaration I had made in that empty building in July 2007. We decided that Friday, August 8, 2008, was the best day to start moving desks, chairs, people, computers, and inventory into the new building. Everyone discussed the order of moving into the new building over Friday, Saturday, and Sunday of that weekend.

Once again, **the power of the words spoken in a declaration over circumstances was driving the timetable for the move into the new building.** I didn't need to remember my words. We actually began moving many things into the building before July 31, 2008, and so we were occupying it by that date. Just as Job 22:28 promised, the light was shining on our ways.

You shall also decree a thing, and it shall be established unto you:
and the light shall shine upon your ways.
—Job 22:28 American KJV

In order to move into the building, we needed a contractor to do the remodel. We did not have one. The economy in Odessa had begun to surge and contractors were hard to find. I called our friend who sold us the building, and he recommended a man to call. I called the man, Alex Acosta, and he immediately went to work on the remodel. Alex did a tremendous job and had the building ready for our move on August 8, 2008. Alex even worked on the July 4 holiday. Again, the power of those words spoken in the declaration seemed to be driving the timetable of our move.

There were several acts of faith that were important to removing the barriers from our path.

Giving, praying, fasting, speaking God's Word over circumstances, making a declaration, praising God in spite of appearances, and submitting a written petition to God were all acts of faith. Some acts of faith were for specific portions of our business and some were for the entire business.

It would be difficult to say that one act of faith was more important than another in removing the barriers. I prefer to say that all of our acts of faith were manifesting out of hearts that were totally trusting in God and His power to deliver us out of adverse circumstances. What was most important in moving the barriers were our hearts . . . hearts totally convinced of the power of God and His promises in His Word.

WHAT IS FAITH?

Faith is a word that is used a lot, and every once in a while it helps me to review its definition in my mind and reflect on its meaning. This is a good place to do that, and Scripture will give us the proper perspective on faith. In the Bible, Hebrews 11:1 defines faith. Here are three translations of that verse:

*Now faith is the **substance** of things hoped for,*
the evidence of things not seen;
—Hebrews 11:1 American KJV

*Now faith is **confidence** in what we hope for and assurance*
about what we do not see; — Hebrews 11:1 NIV

*Now faith brings our hopes into reality and becomes the **foundation***
needed to acquire the things we long for. It is all the evidence
required to prove what is still unseen.
— Hebrews 11:1 TPT

In addition to defining what faith is, Scripture also tells us how we acquire faith.

*. . . according as **God has dealt** to every man the measure of faith.*
—*Romans 12:3b American KJV*

*. . . in accordance with the faith **God has distributed** to each of you.*
—*Romans 121:3b NIV*

Scripture also tells us how to increase or grow our faith if we desire.

*So then **faith comes** by hearing, and hearing by the word of God.*
—*Romans 10:17 American KJV*

*Consequently, **faith comes** from hearing the message, and the message is heard through the word about Christ.*
—*Romans 10:17 NIV*

FAITH SUMMARY

So paraphrasing the above Scriptures, God has given a determined amount of faith to each one of us and we can grow our faith if we listen to God's Word. **Said differently, if I routinely expose myself to hearing God's Word, similar to routinely exercising in a gym to increase muscle tone, I will grow the amount of faith that God has given me.**

Faith is a spiritual substance that can become a physical substance. In the heavenly realm, faith exists as a spiritual substance. When we release faith into the natural realm, it becomes a physical substance fixing what is broken or becoming what we speak. When we pray, speak, or do an act of faith, we release spiritual substance into the circumstance and it actually becomes physical substance.

The amount of spiritual substance you are able to release can be increased by listening to God's Word.

THE POWER OF FAITH

Jesus describes faith as like a seed in one Scripture, and He said that just as a seed can grow into a big plant, so can your faith grow into something larger.

He replied, "If you have faith as small as a mustard seed, you can say to this mulberry tree, 'Be uprooted and planted in the sea,' and it will obey you." —Luke 17:6 NIV

An act of faith can be a behavior or statement made contrary to the reality of current circumstances. An act of faith comes out of confidence that God sees our circumstances differently than we do, and that what looks impossible to us looks very simple to Him. When we know God's promises, His way of doing things, and the precedents established in the Bible in similar situations, we can be confident that He will respond similarly in our situation. An act of faith is usually totally opposite to what our "natural realm" reasoning would dictate. An act of faith may defy natural reasoning and may even appear irrational. An act of faith requires your realization that **circumstances are subordinate to the power of God released by your behavior or statement of faith**. Confidence that God will miraculously move on your behalf is faith. Faith gives us **pivotal advantages** in life.

Kara and I are convinced that our demonstrations of faith brought God's infinite power to prevail against adverse circumstances.

Circumstances do not always appear changed the moment our faith is released. When the declaration from Job 22:28 was spoken, we now know, the light began shining on our ways at that moment. Even though it looked like nothing was happening in the physical realm, even though the circumstances looked unchanged, God was making things happen in the unseen spirit realm. As we gave, blessings were being given to us as is stated in Luke 6:38. As everyone prayed, God's answers to those prayers began happening in the unseen realm at the moment people began praying. The moment the petition was submitted to the Court of Heaven, a judgment was issued in favor of Pharmacy Unlimited. Acts of faith please God. Every act of faith made a difference, from the moment it was released.

Nathan and Alana had been marketing to a large account in Lubbock that owned a chain of nursing homes. In September 2008, the account decided to come onto service with Pharmacy Unlimited. When we added all of their locations over the months of November and December 2008, they increased our business by 50 percent. The Light of God had shined on Pharmacy Unlimited one more time, and one more time, a threat to our existence disappeared because of what came out of our mouths.

REFLECTION

On September 1, 2007, Pharmacy Unlimited had lost 48 percent of its business and was losing money. By December 1, 2008, Pharmacy Unlimited had regained that 48 percent of business *and* had gained an increase above that of 50 percent more business—and we were operating in a new building. And we were profitable.

Here is another interesting thing: in the early months of 2008, an oil boom had begun in Odessa, and when oil booms start, all available people seek employment in the oil fields. As we entered September 2007, we could not see that our need to reduce staff was temporary—it only lasted three months. If we had dismissed our trained staff, instead of hanging onto them even though we were losing money, it would have been very difficult to handle the return of all the lost business in the last part of 2007 and early part of 2008 or the increase in business in the last part of 2008. The Lord was guiding us, regarding staffing of Pharmacy Unlimited, even before we were aware of circumstances.

We have just recalled events from January 2, 2001 through December 31, 2008, a span of seven years. It has been humbling to revisit all of these events. These pages are full of miracles that came as a result of God hearing and responding to three things: our praises to Him, His promises spoken over our circumstances, and our prayers to Him.

The events from January 2, 2001 through December 31, 2008 answer the questions presented in Chapter Two: 1) Does God still do miracles today? and 2) Will God do a miracle for us? The answers are accentuated in this story. God wants to do the same thing for anyone . . . especially for you.

God did the same thing for a harlot who lived in a doomed city and He did the same thing for a young widow born in a country that God had cursed.

Here is how that is expressed in the Bible:

Peter said, "Now I know for certain that God doesn't show favoritism with people but treats everyone on the same basis." —Acts 10:34 TPT

The footnote to this Scripture in *The Passion Translation* is quoted verbatim here: *"The Greek is 'God is not One who receives masks (faces).' God doesn't treat us according to externalities but according to what is in our hearts."*

Here are two answers for anyone:
1) *Yes*, God still does miracles today, and
2) God will do miracles for you!

Six

PUT YOUR MONEY WHERE YOUR MOUTH IS

Early in 2009, we made a collective decision with staff to buy new operating software for the Pharmacy. We installed the software for our entire operation in June of 2009. To say that the installation was a nightmare is an understatement. It was a horrible experience that produced horrible results. By the time we stopped using the software over a year later, we had lost all of our profitability for an entire fiscal year. Certainly, we did not make a bad decision intentionally. We thought we were making a good decision. Let us give this software the name "Interruption" because that is what it did to us. It interrupted us from taking care of business and it interrupted our profitability.

We bought Interruption because it would not only replace the operating software we were using, it would also replace an archiving software we had purchased three years earlier. Let us call the archiving software "Dependable." Though Dependable was very functional, user friendly, and had enhanced our operation, I thought Dependable's maintenance contract was expensive; so if we could replace Dependable and our current operating software with Interruption, we could get rid of Dependable's expensive maintenance contract. We thought we had a good plan to combine two software programs and reduce cost.

In October 2009, payment was due on the maintenance contract for Dependable. We had agreed to a five-year maintenance contract of $15,000 per year due each October. I decided I would let the company that sold us Dependable know I was not going to pay the maintenance contract any more. After all, we were going to combine two software programs and eliminate the need for Dependable. Our contact with Dependable was a godly lady named Mileen. She was very kind to me. She didn't complain in any way. She just wished us well.

God began dealing with me about breaking the maintenance contract I had signed with Dependable. Over the next four to six weeks, I became more and more uncomfortable about not honoring the contract I had signed. Kara had not felt good about breaking the contract, but I was going to save that $15,000 and I really did not want to hear what anyone else had to say about it. However, God kept bothering me about the integrity of my word. I was counting on His Word to have integrity, but I had removed the integrity of my word by breaking that contract. I knew I had to restore integrity to my word.

Our son, Jeremy, joined Pharmacy Unlimited in September 2009. Jeremy's background brought much-needed expertise in several areas, especially data collecting and analysis. Jeremy's abilities enlarged our foundation, improved our product for clients, and improved our operation. Jeremy took charge of IT and became very knowledgeable of how Interruption worked. His insights into how Interruption had been developed let us know quickly that things would never improve. We had to find another operating software to remedy the bad purchase we had made.

In early December 2009, I called Mileen and told her that I was sending a check for $15,000. I let her know that God had been dealing with me. She was so kind, and in our conversation she learned that we had purchased Interruption. She was very concerned for us, and she contacted the owner of another software company and got us acquainted with him. We planned a trip to Indiana, to a pharmacy using the recommended software.

In early 2010, Jeremy, Kara, and I went to two cities in Indiana to look at pharmacies using two different brands of software, the brand Mileen had recommended as well as another brand. The visit was insightful and we returned home to finalize our purchase decision and conversion. Kara and Jeremy made the decision on our new software purchase and we planned the conversion to new software to begin in July 2010. This time we installed one client at a time. It was a very safe and controlled conversion to a new software. Incidentally, Mileen had recommended the brand we chose. We continued to use Dependable. And we were careful about the integrity of our word.

It took several months for the installation to be completed, but it was done smoothly and correctly. It drastically improved our operation. Kara and Jeremy had "hit a home run" in the selection of the software. And, as we converted each client's account to the new software, problems diminished and full profitability returned.

Decisions had to be made during the conversion process, and one of those decisions caused a very large problem three years down the road. It's not something we knew would happen at the time.

In August 2009, a client in San Antonio arranged a meeting with their good friend who was opening a new rehabilitation and nursing facility. Upon meeting this friend, Tim Crank, I discovered that we had many things in common. Tim's building was under construction and would not be operational for several months, but we reached an agreement to serve his facility when it opened.

Tim Crank and his partners opened the new San Antonio facility in May 2010, and he and his partners were on a growth track to open at least five new facilities over the next three years. In our discussions about how Pharmacy Unlimited would handle his account, I personally told Tim that we would do things a certain way, and each month I monitored his account to make sure things happened the way we had agreed. Things went well, Tim was happy with us, and our business with Tim and his partners grew as they continued on their growth track.

In June of 2011, our son, Nathan, had completed pharmacy school, and he moved back to Odessa to join the business. As was the case with Jeremy, Nathan's background brought needed expertise in several areas. Nathan took charge of marketing and client relations; therefore, he began making routine business reviews with our clients, and it was in one of these routine client reviews, two years later, that a huge problem was uncovered.

In August 2013, Nathan and his family moved to San Antonio. We were sensing that we needed a presence in San Antonio, and upon moving, he began making all the preparations to open a second branch of Pharmacy Unlimited in San Antonio. As things progressed over the next year, we realized we needed to move the entire pharmacy operation to San Antonio rather than operate two pharmacy locations.

SURPRISE BARRIER

In September 2013, Nathan conducted a business review with Tim Crank. A question arose during the business review in San Antonio, and Nathan called me in Odessa to reference how Tim Crank's facilities had been set up and were being billed. When I checked the setup in our new software, I discovered that we had been accidentally overcharging all of Tim's facilities since converting his facilities to the new software. At the least, the possibility of overcharging a client was an embarrassing discovery, but we would find that there was much more to it. We informed Tim, apologized, and scheduled a meeting in two weeks to discuss Tim's question.

Our calculations over the next week to ten days revealed that our overcharging of Tim's facilities amounted to a number that was six figures in size and was worth about half of our annual profit from operations. Not only were we embarrassed by this happening, the correction was going to have a big impact on our operation. Nonetheless, we made sure that all of our calculations were correct, as we prepared the information for the meeting with Tim and his staff.

As you can imagine, Nathan and I were devastated by the amount of the overcharge, the impact of repayment, and the damage to our client's trust in us. We found ourselves in a situation where we could rationalize taking a less than honest approach—where situational ethics could be used to justify withholding all or part of the money from the client. One temptation was, "You can report part of it and keep part of it because you need it." Another temptation was, "He has gotten along without it and it would hurt our business to credit all of that money back to our client." These rationalizations suggested to us that we might be justified to be less than honest.

However, we knew that any effort to protect our cash flow that violated a universal law would have an effect opposite of what we desired. Trying to preserve our cash by being dishonest would actually cause a loss of profitability. Because of a universal law that we could not see, we would get the opposite of what our reasoning suggested. By trying to preserve our cash flow dishonestly, we felt that we would actually decrease our cash flow.

Our business was not founded upon compromised principles and laws. We knew that we had to handle this issue according to the foundation that had been laid under our business. Also, in spite of the devastating situation, we had an inner peace that God would take care of us as we did the right thing. Below are five Scriptures that are part of our foundation:

You shall not steal. (One of the Ten Commandments)
—Exodus 20:15 NIV

You shall not give false testimony against your neighbor.
—Exodus 20:16 NIV

*The Lord detests dishonest scales, but **accurate weights find favor with Him**. —Proverbs 11:1 NIV*

The Lord detests differing weights, and dishonest scales do not please Him. —Proverbs 20:23 NIV

People do not despise a thief if he steals to satisfy his hunger when he is starving. Yet if he is caught, he must pay sevenfold, though it costs him all the wealth of his house. —Proverbs 6:30-31 NIV

The overcharge situation was a barrier not so much for survival, but a barrier to maintaining the foundation built under our business. A foundation established upon universal laws will always be solid. If a foundation has compromises such as situational ethics built into it, then the consequences of those compromises weaken that foundation. If a foundation cracks from flaws within it, a building supported by that foundation can collapse.

Below is a look at a very common application of a universal law.

A VISIBLE EFFECT FROM AN INVISIBLE UNIVERSAL LAW

Orville and Wilbur Wright became famous for breaking the barrier for a power-driven, heavier-than-air machine to fly. They built the first successful airplane in the world and had four successful flights on December 3, 1903. They did this by applying Bernoulli's Principle (hereafter referred to as BP) to the wing design of their airplane. Bernoulli's Principle states that "the higher the speed of a flowing fluid or gas, the lower the pressure. As the speed decreases, the pressure increases."

This principle was observed by a Swiss mathematician named Daniel Bernoulli in the 1700s. His observations were made with water flowing in streams, rivers, and tubes. The barrier to man learning to fly was determining how to correctly apply BP, an invisible law, to the shape of an airplane wing. The top surface of the wing must have an upward curve that is higher on the leading edge of the wing and lower on the trailing edge of the wing (causing air to move faster and therefore lowering pressure on the topside of the wing). The bottom surface of the wing is flat with no curvature (causing air to move slower under the bottom side of the wing and increasing pressure or creating lift).

After building a wind tunnel and testing over 200 wing shapes in the wind tunnel, the Wright brothers solved most of the problems of lift and balance in flight.[9]

Though Daniel Bernoulli observed the principle, God spoke it into being. Though you do not see the BP at work on the wing surfaces of an airplane, what God spoke into being as a law of the universe works any time air moves over the wing surfaces. The BP is consistent; it is in effect all the time. In other words, it is not situational. It is not a "works one day and not the next day" law; it is a law in effect every minute of every day, year after year after year; and, it is a law that works for anyone. It is universal, just like all of God's laws.

Said differently, God's laws are absolute. They are in effect all the time, they work all the time, and they work the same for any person, regardless of who the person might be. So, when any pilot gets into an airplane to fly, he does not have to flip a switch to turn on the BP so he can fly. The BP will cause any airplane with proper wing design to fly any time, even though no one sees the universal law at work.

Proper foundation design using universal laws will cause any business, household, government agency, church, or marriage to prosper. Trials may come that test the foundation, but if it is built with universal laws, it will withstand any trial.

The meeting day arrived, and Nathan and I went into that meeting feeling very humble. An associate of Tim's was also in the meeting with us. We presented all the information, showed the overcharge, explained that the overcharge began accruing when we changed software, and presented a plan to them for the repayment of the overcharge. Though the overcharge had taken place for three years in some of Tim's facilities, we would repay the amounts monthly over the next year. And that is exactly what we did.

Tim was very gracious. As we reviewed the overcharges by month and by facility, he listened. When we presented our plan for crediting the overcharge, he approved of our plan. Nathan and I left that meeting grateful for Tim's sympathetic understanding. In addition, it is hard to describe the peace we felt as we left that meeting.

Profoundly, we credited all of the overcharges on schedule as agreed without any memorable hardship to our cash flow.

RELOCATION

With the decision made to move Pharmacy Unlimited's operations to San Antonio, we began planning the move. When the preparations for the move were completed, we moved the production part of our operation from Odessa to San Antonio, a distance of 340 miles, and we did it overnight. We closed for the day on a Friday night in Odessa, and opened for business the next day, Saturday, in San Antonio. That was quite an undertaking. Half of our pharmacy staff made the move to San Antonio. The date of the move was September 19, 2014.

Our business office remained in Odessa, so we had two offices. Jeremy installed a good phone system and computer system so both offices were connected but could operate independently of each other in case of power or phone line interruptions. Things were set up very well and we began dispensing out of our pharmacy site in San Antonio.

In the months and years after our move to San Antonio, Pharmacy Unlimited's business more than doubled. Certainly, our location was an influencing factor in our growth. We believe, though, that we had some universal laws giving lift to our business, just as Bernoulli's Principle gives lift to the wings of an airplane.

We applied three laws daily to our circumstances, and they were just as invisible as the BP causing an airplane to fly. These are the three laws:

1. God inhabits the praises of His people;

2. God's Words spoken into circumstances with a believing heart produce what He intended the spoken words to produce;

3. Our tongues have the power to build or destroy.

These three laws, like the BP, do not have to be activated . . . they are in force all the time. They are laws—so they always work the same way, and they work for all people.

Seven

THE FINAL BARRIER

In mid-2019, Kara and I were having lunch with our sons Jeremy and Nathan. We were discussing the history of Pharmacy Unlimited, and we summed up our history with these words: **"What we have came out of our mouths!"**

All of the impossible negative circumstances that we encountered in the history of Pharmacy Unlimited were changed into blessing by the words of our mouths. We spoke God's promises (what He has spoken by His mouth and recorded in the Bible) into our circumstances, and our circumstances changed to be what was spoken out of our mouths. This is a profound truth.

Going forward, our future is governed by the same revelation.

What we will have in the future will come out of our mouths.

If we speak God's promises over our business, His promises will shape the future of our business. Awesome! And the same is true for you.

A city that was well fortified, and thought to be well able to defend itself against any enemy attack, was defeated *just by words spoken out of the mouths of an army.*

In Joshua 6:2, God told Joshua that He had given Jericho and its king into Israel's hand; this was a promise, and to receive God's promise of victory with Jericho, Joshua and Israel had to follow God's instructions. And they did. The Israelites marched around the city of Jericho without speaking, once daily for six days, and on day seven they marched around the city, without speaking a word, seven times. After the seventh trip around Jericho, the men of Israel shouted and the walls of the city were driven all the way into the ground. The promise of the Lord manifested when they shouted with their mouths.

YOUR WORDS OF FAITH HAVE POWER

I want to encourage you with this thought: Regardless of how things are going for you right now, follow God's example and speak good things into your circumstances. It is interesting that God instructed the men in the army of Israel not to say anything as they walked around the city of Jericho. It is easy to imagine their thoughts as they walked around Jericho: "Look, the walls are so thick that people have houses built into the walls of the city;" "Look how tall the walls are. How will we ever scale those walls to conquer the city?" "What weapon can defeat such a strong, well-fortified city?" Since none of those words that described what was visible were allowed to be spoken by Israel's army, only the words God spoke to Joshua (promises) were released: "God has given us the city and its inhabitants!" God's Word, when spoken by the army of Israel in a shout to the Lord, actually pressed the walls of Jericho into the earth so that Jericho was no longer fortified. Can you imagine the total shock to the citizens of Jericho when their fortress was suddenly gone? If you speak God's promises into your circumstances, believing that your circumstances will change into what you speak, it will happen.

What you are and what you have came out of your mouth. What you will be and what you will have will come out of your mouth.

You may have heard people say there are always two ways of doing anything . . . the wrong way and the right way. We won't argue that in this book. However, there are two methods for approaching negative circumstance in your life: 1) It is possible to change circumstances with our human methods; or 2) It is possible to change circumstances by doing it God's way.

Our way of doing things is by our strength, our plans, our understanding, and our hard work . . . all of which have limitations. **God's way of doing things is to change circumstances by speaking His promises into those circumstances . . . none of which have limitations.** This is another **pivotal revelation about life.**

Centuries ago, there was a couple who had become old without having children. Throughout their lives, they were unable to conceive. God spoke a promise to the man that he would have a son in his old age, even though he and his wife were past the time when it was possible to conceive a child. That man was Abram in the book of Genesis in the Bible. When God gave Abram the promise, He (God) also changed Abram's name. The effect of the name change was that Abram began speaking God's promise any time he spoke his name, because his new name was Abraham, which means "father of many nations." Abraham's circumstances—having no children from Sarah, his wife—changed when he spoke God's promise into his circumstances.

Precedents in Scripture are codes. They establish God's heart and His outlook toward certain things. Scripture has established powerful precedents for transforming circumstances to victory by what is spoken out of our mouths. Just as Rahab and Ruth were transformed from reproach to honor, Abraham and Joshua saw victory over impossible barriers by speaking God's promises into circumstances. These precedents serve as examples for us when we encounter barriers. God's precedents establish that barriers cannot stand against His promises spoken against them.

THE ULTIMATE BARRIER BREAKTHROUGH

There is a barrier for entry into Heaven. That barrier is sin. God has defined sin, the barrier, in Scripture. We cannot fully comprehend the barrier of sin by opinions. Sin is part of our DNA, as well as part of our behavior. We have no power to remove sin . . . but removing sin is required to receive salvation and go to Heaven.

There is only one way to remove that barrier. It has to be removed by God, and God has provided a way for us to remove that barrier through His Son's death and resurrection.

Jesus provided a way for our sin (the barrier preventing entry into Heaven) to be washed away by His righteous blood being poured out on the way to the cross and upon the cross. Jesus literally suffered the loss of all of His blood to take away the sin of the world. As Jesus died on the cross, our sin was placed on the blood of His beaten and bloody body. As He died, our sin was removed.

As He was resurrected from death, He made new life available to us, free from the barrier of sin.

Jesus' blood and resurrection removed the barrier of sin for us. This is a promise from God. According to precedent, the promise is activated by what we speak. As we speak with our mouths the promise that the sin barrier is removed, our circumstances of sin and who we are in sin are changed. Just as a prostitute doomed for destruction and a young widow born under a curse were redeemed out of their circumstances by what they spoke, so we are redeemed from the circumstances of sin by what we speak. If you will believe, accept, and speak the promise of God mentioned in this paragraph, you will transform your spirit supernaturally. Here is a prayer to help you speak the promise of the redeeming power of Jesus' blood into the sinful circumstances in which you were born and in which you have behaved:

Lord Jesus, I believe that You are the Son of God, a Son of promise born into the world as a man, so that You could give Your blood to take away my sin as You died on the cross. Lord Jesus, I accept the free gift of Your blood to take away my sin, past, present, and future. I speak out loud with my mouth that I believe this and accept it for myself. I speak into my circumstances of sin that I am now cleansed of all sin by Your blood. I invite You to live in my spirit from now on. I speak into my circumstances that I am a new being through Your redeeming power. Just as Rahab and Ruth were transformed, I speak that I am now transformed by Your promise and Your power. And just as You died on the cross and were raised from the dead, I believe in my heart and confess with my mouth that death will not have eternal power over me. I speak with my mouth that I will be with You in Heaven. Thank You, Jesus! Amen.

God says that His Words will always come to pass, so God has established a universal law regarding His Words. We are created in the image of God, according to Genesis 1:27, and our tongues have power over life and death, even building or destroying, according to what God spoke in Proverbs 18:21. Is it possible that Genesis 1:27 and Proverbs 18:21 establish that our tongues are governed by universal laws? If so, the power in our tongues is always there, and even though our words are invisible when spoken, they will produce a visible effect . . . just like the BP.

So God created mankind in his own image, in the image of God he created them; male and female he created them.
—Genesis 1:27 NIV

The tongue has the power of life and death, and those who love it will eat its fruit. —Proverbs 18:21 NIV

PRAISE IS A UNIVERSAL LAW FOR SUCCESS

In my opinion, God has established a universal law that He will inhabit our praise. Again, in my opinion, after God has inhabited our praise, words spoken in His presence are energized by God's presence and power.

Praise to God releases power. In Appendix III, you will find the words to the song "Raise a Hallelujah." The lyrics of this song tell of barriers being broken because Heaven fights for you. May the words of this song be your experience. Make your words of praise and blessings be forceful and frequent. Break the barriers that you encounter.

The verse in I Chronicles 16:37-43 records that King David kept over 70 men at the Ark of the Covenant, where the presence of God dwelt in Israel, to praise God continually (bolded text in several places are my additions). King David knew that praise was very, very important for the nation of Israel. From Psalm 22:3, we know that David knew that God inhabits the praises of His people. In addition, we know from Psalm 18:3 that David knew that praising God would save him from his enemies.

*37 So he left there before the ark of the covenant of the Lord Asaph and his brothers, to minister before the ark **continually**, as every day's work required: 38 and Obed-edom with their brothers, threescore and eight; Obed-edom also the son of Jeduthun and Hosah to be porters: 39 And Zadok the priest, and his brothers the priest, before the tabernacle of the Lord in the high place that was at Gibeon, 40 to offer burnt offerings unto the Lord upon the altar of the burnt offering, **continually morning and evening**, and to do according to all that is written in the Law of the Lord, which He commanded Israel; 41 And with them Heman and Jeduthun, and the rest that were chosen, who were expressed by name, to give thanks to the Lord, because His mercy endures for ever; 42 and with them Jeman and Jeduthun with trumpets and cymbals for those that should make a sound, and with musical instruments of God. And the sons of Jeduthun were porters. 43 And all the people departed every man to his house: and David returned to bless his house.*
—I Chronicles 16:37-43 American KJV

You are holy, O You that inhabits the praises of Israel.
—Psalms 22:3 American KJV

I will call upon the Lord, who is worthy to be praised:
so shall I be saved from my enemies.
—Psalm 18:3 American KJV

We all have barriers in our way at some point in life, and those barriers can surely be penetrated by applying God's universal laws to circumstances with our mouths.

The prescription for breakthrough is this:

Apply God's promises through His universal laws to your circumstances by the words of your mouth.

In the inspiring words of Winston Churchill, "Never give up. Never. Never give up."

May God's richest blessings be spoken out of your mouth to change your circumstances into what He desires for you. May you embrace this mystery.

EPILOGUE

This year, on January 2, we quietly celebrated being in business for 20 years as Pharmacy Unlimited. In my heart, I thanked God for His universal laws, His Covenant, and His constant care that have enabled us to survive the threats to our existence in our early years; and now, I am thankful that by His blessings we are thriving. To me, it was an awesome occasion for realizing that we walk in all of the blessings that were once spoken over Pharmacy Unlimited. And it was a humbling occasion to realize our success has come from no strength of ours. Our success is only and totally due to God's powerful blessing on our business. It is by His Word that we have survived and prospered. Thank You, Lord God!

In the words in the above paragraph, please know that I am *not* speaking from a false humility. I am speaking from reality. Anytime I look back over the years and review the path we followed, I am again aware of the miracles of those moments through the years.

Several years later, people would look at our business and brag on our success. They always credited our success to things that could be easily seen in the light of success, such as focus on goals, hard work, dedication, a good business plan, a good vision for the business, and good marketing. Incorporated into the foundation of our business are the images of conquered barriers that once totally blocked our path with messages of impossibility. Also, our foundation incorporates the praises to God, the blessings spoken, and the prayers of desperate need. Those things that were once a threat are now memorials to the source of our strength. When those huge impossibilities are mentioned to onlookers as we tell our story, they appear as a paradox to what is now visible. In our case, a prosperous business hardly looks like it was once starving and nearly died due to lack of capital.

Thank you for reading our story. May the universal laws applied in our story release miracles in your circumstances. May God richly bless your endeavors at breaking barriers and removing obstacles. In addition to the universal laws that we have spoken of, may God reveal others to you. With His power, outcomes are always good. With His power, barriers are truly broken and obstacles are removed. God truly is the *Prescription for Breakthrough*.

ENDNOTES

1. Sheffield, Jack. *God's Healing River.* Morgan Printing: 2003.

2. https://www.quora.com/What-percentage-of-the-light-spectrum-are-humans-able-to-see-with-their-eyes

3. G. & C. Merriam Co., *Webster's Seventh New Collegiate Dictionary.* Rand McNally & Company, Chicago, Illinois.

4. http://www.creationstudies.org/Education/miracles_of_the_bible.html

5. Amaral, Joe. *Understanding Jesus: Cultural Insights into the Words and Deeds of Christ.* FaithWords, Hachette Book Group, New York, New York: 2011.

6. https://www.internationalultrarunning.com/2hourmarathon

7. https://www.smithsonianmag.com/smart-news/five-things-know-about-roger-bannister-first-person-break-four-minute-mile-180968344/

8. Benefiel, Dr. John. *Binding the Strongman Over America: Healing the Land, Transferring Wealth, and Advancing the Kingdom of God.* Benefiel Ministries, Incorporated, Oklahoma City, Oklahoma: 2012.

9. World Book Encyclopedia, 1984, W, X, Y, Z Volume, pp. 420-421; and World Book Encyclopedia, 1984, B Volume, p. 211.

10. Heiser, Jonathan David. Skaggs, Molly. Stevens, Jake. *Raise a Hallelujah*; Songwriters: Jonathan David Heiser, Molly Skaggs, Jake Stevens; Published by Bethel Music Publishing. Source: LyricFind.

APPENDIX I

EXAMPLES OF PRAISE

1. I praise You, Lord, because You are a shield for me. I praise You, Lord, because You are my glory and the lifter of my head. (Psalm 3:3 American KJV)

2. I praise You, Lord, because You hear my voice when I cry out to You. (Psalm 3:4 American KJV)

3. I praise You, God of my righteousness, because You have enlarged me when I was in distress. (Psalm 4:1 American KJV)

4. I praise You, Lord, because with my heart I believe to righteousness and with the confession of my mouth I am saved. (Romans 10:10 American KJV)

5. I praise You, Lord, because You have made me Your righteousness. (II Corinthians 5:21 American KJV)

6. I praise You, Lord, because You will bless the righteous and You will surround him with favor like a shield. (Psalm 5:12 American KJV)

7. I praise You, O Lord my Lord, because Your name is the most excellent name in all the earth! I praise You, Lord, because You have set Your glory above the heavens. (Psalm 8:1 American KJV)

8. I praise You, Lord, because You have made man in Your image and after Your likeness. (Genesis 1:26 American KJV)

9. I praise You, Lord, because You are a refuge for me in times of trouble. (Psalm 9:9 American KJV)

10. I praise You, Lord, because You have not forsaken me because I seek You. (Psalm 9:10 American KJV)

11. I praise You, Lord, because You do not forget my humble cry. (Psalm 9:12 American KJV)

12. I praise You, Lord, because You are King forever. (Psalm 10:16 American KJV)

13. I praise You, Lord, because Your Words are pure like silver purified in the fire seven times. (Psalm 12:6 American KJV)

14. I praise You, Lord, because You have dealt bountifully with me. (Psalm 13:6 American KJV)

15. I praise You, Lord, because You show me the path of life. (Psalm 16:11 American KJV)

16. I praise You, Lord, because fullness of joy is in Your presence and at Your right hand there are pleasures for evermore. (Psalm 16:11 American KJV)

17. I praise You, Lord, because in my distress I called upon You and You heard my voice out of Your temple. (Psalm 18:6 American KJV)

18. I praise You, Lord, because You will keep my lamp burning and You will turn my darkness into light. (Psalm 18:28 NIV)

19. I praise You, Lord God, because You make Your saving help my shield, and Your right hand sustains me. (Psalm 18:35 NIV)

20. I praise You, Lord God, because Your help has made me great. (Psalm 18:35 American KJV)

21.   I praise You, Lord, because You have armed me with strength for battle and You have humbled my adversaries before me. (Psalm 8:39 NIV)

22.   I praise You, Lord, because the heavens declare Your glory and the skies proclaim the work of Your hands. (Psalm 19:1 American KJV)

23.   I praise You, Lord, because You give victory to me and You answer me from Your heavenly sanctuary with the victorious power of Your right hand. (Psalm 20:6 American KJV)

24.   I praise You, Lord, because You are holy and You inhabit the praises of Your people. (Psalm 22:3 American KJV)

25.   I praise You, Lord God, because You are the King of Glory! I praise You, Lord, because You are strong and mighty in battle. (Psalm 24:8 American KJV)

26.   I praise You, Lord, because You are the God of my salvation. (Psalm 25:5 American KJV)

27.   I praise You, Lord God, because You are my light and my salvation and You are the strength of my life. (Psalm 27:1 American KJV)

28.   I praise You, Lord God, because in the time of trouble You will hide me in Your pavilion and the secret of Your tabernacle. (Psalm 27:5 American KJV)

29.   I praise You, Lord, because You are my strength and shield. (Psalm 28:7 American KJV)

30.   I praise You, Lord, because You have lifted me out of the depths and did not let my enemies gloat over me. (Psalm 30:1 NIV)

31.   I praise You, Lord, because You brought me up from the realm of the dead; You spared me from going down to the pit. (Psalm 30:3 NIV)

32. I praise You, Lord, because You are my hiding place and You preserve me from trouble. (Psalm 32:7 American KJV)

33. I praise You, Lord, because You surround me with songs of deliverance. (Psalm 32:7 American KJV)

34. I praise You, Lord, because You surround me with mercy because I trust in You. (Psalm 32:10 American KJV)

35. I praise You, Lord God, because by Your Word the heavens were made and all the stars by the breath of Your mouth. (Psalm 33:6 NIV)

36. I praise You, Lord, because Your plans stand firm forever, and the purposes of Your heart through all generations. (Psalm 33:11 American KJV)

37. I praise You, Lord, because Your eyes are on me because I fear You and hope in Your unfailing love to deliver me from death and keep me alive during famine. (Psalm 33:18-19 American KJV)

38. I praise You, Lord, because I sought You and You answered me and delivered me from all of my fears. (Psalm 34:4 NIV)

39. I praise You, Lord, because I cry out and You hear me and deliver me from all of my troubles. (Psalm 34:17 NIV)

40. I praise You, Lord, because though I may have many troubles, You deliver me from all of them and You protect all of my bones so that not one of them is broken. (Psalm 34:19-20 NIV)

APPENDIX II

EXAMPLES OF BLESSINGS TO SPEAK

1. I bless me to walk in the advice and habits of godly people. (Psalm 1:1 American KJV)

2. I bless me to be like a tree planted by streams of water, which yields its fruit in season, and whose leaves do not wither, so that whatever I do prospers. (Psalm 1:3 NIV)

3. I bless me to keep the Lord's Word in my mouth all the time and I bless me to meditate on the Lord's Word day and night so that my ways may prosper and I have great success. (Joshua 1:8 American KJV)

4. I bless me to fear the Lord, my God, to walk in all His ways, and to love Him and serve Him with all my heart and soul. (Deuteronomy 10:12 American KJV)

5. I bless me to be blessed in the city and blessed in the country. (Deuteronomy 28:3 NIV)

6. I bless me to see God's blessings on the fruit of my body, the fruit of my ground, my livestock, and my basket and store. (Deuteronomy 28:4-5 American KJV)

7. I bless me to be blessed when I come in and when I go out. (Deuteronomy 28:6 American KJV)

8. I bless me to have the enemies who rise up against me to be smitten before God's face so that they come out against me one way and flee before me seven ways. (Deuteronomy 28:7 American KJV)

9. I bless me to have the Lord send blessings upon my barns, my bank accounts, my investments, and everything I put my hand to. (Deuteronomy 28:8 NIV)

10. I bless me to be established by the Lord as a holy people. (Deuteronomy 28: 9 American KJV)

11. I bless me to be recognized by all the peoples of the earth as called by the name of the Lord and protected by Him. (Deuteronomy 28:10 NIV)

12. I bless me to have the Lord grant me abundant prosperity in my family, my investments, and all that I put my hand to. (Deuteronomy 28:11 NIV)

13. I bless me to have the Lord open the heavens and the storehouse of His bounty upon me. (Deuteronomy 28:12 NIV)

14. I bless me to have the Lord send rain upon my land in season and to bless all the work of my hands. (Deuteronomy 28:12 NIV)

15. I bless me to be so blessed by the Lord that I lend to many nations but will borrow from none. (Deuteronomy 28:12 NIV)

16. I bless me to be made the head and not the tail by the Lord because I pay attention to the Word of the Lord. (Deuteronomy 28:13 NIV)

17. I bless me to always be at the top and never at the bottom because I never turn aside from the Word of the Lord. (Deuteronomy 28:13-14 NIV)

18. I bless me to seek You, Lord, because my soul thirsts for You. (Psalm 63:1 American KJV)

19. I bless me to see Your power and Your glory, Lord. (Psalm 63:2 American KJV)

20. I bless me to praise You, Lord, with my lips and to lift up my hands in Your name. (Psalm 63:3-4 American KJV)

21. I bless me to hear the Word of God so that my faith increases. (Romans 10:17 American KJV)

22. I bless me to walk in faith, always. (II Corinthians 5:7 American KJV)

ANCIENT CODES FOR BREAKTHROUGH

1. God created us to be like Him . . . a mirror image of Him.

2. Jesus has redeemed us to be like God.

3. God knows what is going on in your life and He wants to help.

4. God's promises have His power in them. We release that power when we speak His promises.

5. Our mouths have the power to build or destroy. When we bless, we build.

6. God speaks with the success of His Word in mind when He speaks.

7. God sees us through what His Word says.

8. Praise connects us to God.

9. God is inclusive, not exclusive. God wants to include you in His Kingdom rather than exclude you.

10. Look for precedents to build your confidence that God will answer your prayer. If He has done something once, He will do it again. The stories of Rahab and Ruth are precedents.

11. A precedent is a platform upon which you can stand and have God's favor as you pray.

12. Faith is a substance that releases God's power and the power of His Word into our need. Faith gives us ownership of what we ask for.

APPENDIX III

RAISE A HALLELUJAH[10]

I raise a hallelujah, in the presence of my enemies
I raise a hallelujah, louder than the unbelief
I raise a hallelujah, my weapon is a melody
I raise a hallelujah, heaven comes to fight for me

I'm gonna sing, in the middle of the storm
Louder and louder, you're gonna hear my praises roar
Up from the ashes, hope will arise
Death is defeated, the King is alive!

I raise a hallelujah, with everything inside of me
I raise a hallelujah, I will watch the darkness flee
I raise a hallelujah, in the middle of the mystery
I raise a hallelujah, fear you lost your hold on me!

I'm gonna sing, in the middle of the storm
Louder and louder, you're gonna hear my praises roar
Up from the ashes, hope will arise
Death is defeated, the King is alive!

Sing a little louder (In the presence of my enemies)
Sing a little louder (Louder than the unbelief)

Sing a little louder (My weapon is a melody)
Sing a little louder (Heaven comes to fight for me)
Sing a little louder (In the presence of my enemies)
Sing a little louder (Louder than the unbelief)
Sing a little louder (My weapon is a melody)
Sing a little louder (Heaven comes to fight for me)
Sing a little louder!

I'm gonna sing, in the middle of the storm
Louder and louder, you're gonna hear my praises roar
Up from the ashes, hope will arise
Death is defeated, the King is alive!

Songwriters: Jonathan David Heiser, Molly Skaggs, Jake Stevens
Published by Bethel Music Publishing
Source: LyricFind

ACKNOWLEDGMENTS

Four men have had a powerful and positive impact on my life. Their influence on me has shaped my life and my outcomes. I am very grateful to each one of them. They deserve honor for the great men they are.

My dad, **Fred Skaggs,** had a heart inclined toward the Lord and he walked by the Spirit of the Lord. The hardships and difficulties my dad endured in the early years of his life had long-lasting influence. His encounters with Jesus Christ enabled him to overcome the shortcomings that resulted from those years. My dad was a giver and demonstrated the principles of giving to me. Roger Lowe described my dad as a man "who walked his talk." With this acknowledgement, I want to bless his memory and his dedicated life.

I went to work for **Roger Lowe** when I was 33 years old and worked for him for 17 years. He has been a great influence on my life because I was able to watch him be a godly husband and father, godly businessman, and godly confidant. Roger is a man after God's own heart, just as King David was in the Bible, except Roger does not have any of the sins King David did. Roger's example of humility and brilliance is a standard of excellence that still inspires me.

Don Palmer was the first pastor I had who was not afraid to talk about the everyday, gritty details of living and how biblical principles could be successfully applied to avoid pitfalls. He taught me the difference between having a relationship with the Lord and having a religious spirit. He taught me to pray Scripture over circumstances, to bless circumstances and people, the principles of praise, and how to read Scripture for what it says versus a doctrinal adaptation. It was his teaching that inspired us to apply the universal laws against our negative circumstances.

Jay Mehaffey was a war hero who served in World War II and participated in the Normandy Invasion at Omaha Beach to liberate France from German occupation. Jay was a true friend who showed me how to relax, take a day to play golf, and enjoy a fine meal with wine. Jay would listen to me and was really a second dad to me. I loved the open dialogue we could have together as friends. He very kindly made me aware of my anger in a golf game and that has been an inspiration to me from that moment until now.

Others have also made a difference in my life.

My mother, **Joyce Skaggs,** was a godly lady who always went to the defense of her kids. She would fight to see that her kids had a fair chance and were treated fairly. She taught me manners, grammar, and social skills, and by her example and encouragement, I learned not to be a quitter. She was congenial and flexible with my dad and my siblings, and she truly was a forgiving lady. My mother loved people and enjoyed visiting with all people, made lifelong friends everywhere she lived, and was always eager to help anyone in need. She always wanted to write and did write a book about her experiences in childhood. As I have written this book, I have thought about her quite a bit. I want to bless her memory and her life, which she dedicated to her family.

The **team members of Pharmacy Unlimited,** past, present, and future, are truly the greatest asset Pharmacy Unlimited has, and they make us better than we would be otherwise. Even though we have invested in a tremendous amount of very costly equipment and technology, our team is what distinguishes us from others in the business. Without our people, we would be a mediocre pharmacy with a lot of expensive equipment and technology. The team members are the ones who stay late, work a day off, work when they're not feeling well, and do amazing things to ensure that a patient gets their medication on time. When our clients brag on Pharmacy Unlimited, they brag about the team. We are blessed to have the past, present, and future team members of Pharmacy Unlimited who all have high character, live with integrity, and are caring, generous, and hardworking people. The Pharmacy Unlimited team truly makes the world a better place by making a difference. God bless you, everyone!

I would also like to acknowledge the book production by Aloha Publishing, AlohaPublishing.com, and the cover and interior design work done by Fusion Creative Works, FusionCW.com.

ABOUT THE AUTHOR

Danny Skaggs has been associated with business all of his adult life. His first job out of pharmacy school was managing a drug store and pharmacy in Austin, Texas. Danny has a private pilot's license and has logged over 2,000 hours as a pilot. He enjoys fishing and hiking in the Rocky Mountains. Pharmacy Unlimited fills prescriptions for nursing homes across the state of Texas.

Danny received his B.S. Pharmacy degree from the University of Texas in Austin. Danny and his wife, Kara, have two sons and two daughters, and have been married 49 years. They are active in their church and reside in San Antonio, Texas.

www.ingramcontent.com/pod-product-compliance
Lightning Source LLC
Chambersburg PA
CBHW031520040426
42445CB00009B/324